GOD'S
LOST
CHILDREN

Letters from Covenant House

Sr. Mary Rose McGeady

Covenant House
1991

DEDICATED
to the
1,000,000
homeless children
who slept on America's streets last year,
scared, cold, hungry, alone,
and most of all,
desperate to find
someone who cares.

Table Of Contents

Introduction

In the time it takes you to read this sentence, a child in America will drop out of school.

In the time it takes you to finish this sentence, another child in this country will run away from home.

In the time it takes you just to read this page, another teenage girl will have a baby.

I suppose by now you understand why I titled this book the way I have. We've reached a time in America when the baby-boomer generation and the "me" generation have been replaced—by a *lost generation*. The sixties flower child has given way to the nineties floundering child. The kid who thinks he or she is invincible (who among us didn't?), has been usurped by a street army of kids who have become invisible. Our country is now gripped by an epidemic of kids who are right now "out there" on America's streets. Lost and alone. Completely on their own.   Hungry. Sick. Scared.

This is a book about these kids—*God's Lost Children*—our lost children.

There are *two things* you should know about these kids before you read another page of this book.

First of all, there's no such thing as a "typical" homeless kid. The kids you'll read about in this book come in all shapes and sizes, from all types of backgrounds, from every kind of religion and in every age group. These kids are boys and girls. They are white, black, and hispanic. They are as young as eight and as "old" as twenty-one. And they come from everywhere—from the north and south, the cities and the suburbs, from the ghettoes and even from America's better neighborhoods.

But as different as they are, they all have one thing in common: none of these kids want to be homeless.

That's the second thing you really need to understand. The kids you'll meet in this book are not out on the street by choice. All too often these kids are homeless because they've literally been thrown out of their houses by parents or stepparents who don't want them or don't care about them. Many others have fled to the street because they were abused at home ... physically, emotionally, continually. For these kids, life at home was so dangerous, they couldn't live there another day.

They are truly victims ... living and breathing symbols of the single greatest tragedy in America this past generation—the complete and tragic breakdown of the American family.

But they can be saved. Yes, you should know that, too. In fact, they are being saved.

Last year, our Covenant House crisis shelters helped rescue 28,000 homeless kids from the street ... boys and girls with no family ... kids who are tired, lonely, hungry, and scared!

When these kids come to our doors, we make a special Covenant with them—an "agreement" among the kids, us, and God. We agree to do all we can to help them and make their life better. They agree to try ... to put their faith in someone or something for the first time.

We give these boys and girls a warm hug and a hot meal. We give them counseling, medicine and clean clothes if they need it (most do). We give them a clean bed to sleep in!

And then, once we've helped a kid get through the night, we help them get on with their lives. For some of these kids, it means getting them in touch with a family member who still cares (if one exists). Or we help them find a job. Or get them into long term drug counseling. Whatever it takes to help these kids we'll give them. Anything.

But most of all, we give thousands of desperate kids something they've never had before. LOVE. Tonight, for the first time ever in their lives, some innocent homeless children will learn that they are loved . . . that their life is truly worth living.

If there's one message you get from this book, I'm praying it is this one. That love truly can save these kids. With enough love—with enough help from good people like you—these kids can be saved. If we just give these kids a foundation of love to build on, they can truly stand up and rise above their hurt and pain, like a phoenix who rises from the ashes.

All this lost generation of kids needs is enough people like you who know about the problem—who understand it—who care about it. That's why I put together this book and I'm praying you'll read it.

Why don't you spend just an hour with me now, and I'll share some amazing—and yes, shocking—stories about who these kids are. Let me show you where these kids come from (the answer may surprise you). How they end up on the street. Why so many of them never make it back. (I should mention that some of these stories are my own—some from our staff who know these kids.)

Just turn this page and step inside the shoes of a homeless kid for sixty minutes. I'll make you this promise—it's a journey you'll remember the rest of your life....

I know none of us at Covenant House will ever forget this first kid, a little girl named Janice....

> In God's love,
> Sister Mary Rose McGeady
> For the Kids

Chapter 1
Janice

She stood on the curb looking scared and lonely and uncomfortable in a skimpy halter top and bright red lipstick.

It was two in the morning. A chilly breeze whipped up the street and seemed to make her shiver. She was just a child.

We pulled our Covenant House van up to the curb, and rolled down the window.

"Hi, what's your name?"

"Janice," she said hesitantly as if she really had to think about her answer.

"Why don't you hop in, Janice? We've got some lemonade and sandwiches. We can talk. You hungry?"

"Yeah, kind of. But not really. I mean, like, I really gotta go. I can't talk now. Maybe later. Will you be back around in a couple hours?"

She glanced nervously up and down the street at the passing cars. We could tell she was dying to jump in, but she was scared. Really scared. The seconds ticked away. . . .

"OK," she finally said. "But only for a minute or two then I gotta go. My boyfriend is gonna be really mad if he finds out I'm doin' this." She climbed in and sat down stiffly across from me.

"Your boyfriend?"

"Yeah, he told me he doesn't want me talking to you guys. So I can't stay long. Can I have a sandwich, too? I'm really hungry."

"Sure, but why do you call him your boyfriend if he lets you walk the street at night? Do you mean your pimp?"

"Oh, no, he's not a pimp, he's my boyfriend," she insisted with dead-serious sincerity. "He loves me. He really does. He buys me a lot of nice things."

After a few weeks on the van, you know when a kid is telling you something to convince you . . . or telling you something to convince herself. In Janice's case, her fingers gave her away.

All the time she spoke, she couldn't stop twisting the cheap-looking ring on her index finger. It was as if she was trying to control herself . . . to lock herself in . . . to stop her from saying something that might get her in trouble.

Finally though, she looked up. And she started to sob.

"I . . . I'm scared, I'm really scared. Do you think you can help me? My boyfriend beats me up sometimes if I don't do what he tells me. I think . . . I think I'm pregnant. Oh God, what am I gonna do?"

We sat there for twenty minutes as Janice's story tumbled out in a torrent of confusion and tears.

She was from Iowa. She'd run away from home after a bad argument with her parents. She'd met her "boyfriend" at the bus station and he promised to take care of her.

But after a few weeks he demanded Janice pay him back for his favors.

"How old are you, Janice," we asked, trying to guess what she would say. She looked maybe seventeen. But the streets can do that to a kid—make them look a lot older than they really are. We waited as she peered out the van window . . . .

"Fourteen," she said, as a steady stream of tears ran down her cheeks. "I've wanted to quit doing this for a long time. But I didn't know how, or where to go. Then I saw your van tonight. I'd heard about it from some of the other girls. I thought maybe you could help. I was afraid to talk to you. I'm really scared my boyfriend's going to find out I'm here and . . . ." her voice trailed off as she quietly sobbed.

"Can we take you back to Covenant House, Janice? We can help you get out of this mess. We'll go right now if you want. We really don't want to see you go out there now that you've come this far. You've been really brave, you know . . . ."

Janice didn't say a word. Finally, she looked at us and nodded her head with what seemed to be a mixture of relief and dread . . . and the van pulled away from the curb and headed back to Covenant House.

As it turned out, Janice was four months pregnant.

And she was even more scared than we realized at first. During her time at Covenant House, she refused to set foot outside even with one of our staff to get some fresh air. She

was petrified her "boyfriend" would see her
and take her back.

Pimps have a lot to lose if their girls leave
them. A typical young prostitute like Janice is
worth thousands and thousands of dollars a
year to her pimp.

But today the only thing Janice is trying to
earn is a new sense of self respect back home in
Iowa. We put her on a plane just a few days
after we picked her up off that street.

I hope and pray that Janice is going to make
it. But the sad thing is, for every kid like Janice
who is rescued off the city streets, there are ten
others out there who'll never get the help they
need. Each year close to one million kids sleep
on the street! 1,000,000! And many of them—
too many of them—are dying out there!

But they don't have to!

That's what this book is all about, and that's
what Covenant House is all about.

Let me tell you about some more of our
kids, so you'll get an idea who these 1,000,000
urban nomads are.

HOW TO DEFUSE
AN ANGRY TEENAGER

No one likes to deal with an angry person, but a certain
amount of teenage anger is inevitable. Often, the key to
success is to understand your child better by finding out
where the anger is coming from, and then adjusting your
own behavior to help your teenager overcome the underlying problems that are causing the anger.

If your child is given to angry outbursts, here are
some suggestions that should help you negotiate a
truce.

Don't panic. Even if you feel that you don't recognize your own child anymore accept it for the
moment.

Listen carefully to what your teenager is blurting
out to you. Try to read between the lines to find out
what the real issue is. Although your teen's insults,
complaints and demands may be hurting you, they
are actually cries for help.

Don't retaliate. Don't come up with threats and
punishments without trying to find out why your teen
is angry. Parental retaliation against teenage anger
often makes the situation worse.

Tell him that he's hurting you—not in such a way
as to make him feel guilty—but in a way that will
make him realize that you're concerned and just trying to understand what's bothering him.

Reexamine the rules. At a non-angry time try to
explain to your teen that although there absolutely
have to be rules in the house, perhaps some of the
"old rules" can be adjusted. Negotiate to develop
rules you can both live with.

Chapter 2
Cindy

"Do you really believe that, Sister? I mean . . . do you really believe it? Do you really believe there's hope for me?"

Her green eyes—scared, empty—darted in to meet mine for only a second, then fell away to the floor.

Cindy was 17, maybe 18. Very small and frail. With curly brown hair and skin which had been burned by too many cold winter nights on the street.

The thing that struck me most, though, was how alone she looked. Even though this young girl stood in the middle of 300 homeless kids in our crisis shelter, she was like a little island, isolated, hard to reach.

I took her hand and bent down to meet her eyes. It was really hard, at a moment like this, not to sound trite. "Of course, there's hope for you," I said. "Covenant House wouldn't be here if I didn't believe that. I wouldn't be here if I didn't believe there was hope for you and every kid here."

Cindy looked away for a moment. Somewhere very, very far away. Her mouth opened just a crack to let a few words escape. "I hope you're right, Sister. I hope so . . . I'll try . . . I hope you're right."

She started to turn away, but I was able to cut off her escape with my left arm, and give her a little hug. She smiled and gave me a hug back. She was way too tired to talk anymore. One of our crisis counselors took her hand, and walked her away. . . .

I still can't believe how young Cindy looked—how frail—how utterly alone.

I suppose that after all the years I've spent working with kids—after 40 exhausting, exhilarating years living and working on the streets with homeless children—I'd get used to moments like this. But you just never do. Seeing a kid hurt like that never stops hurting me.

It helps to know, however, that with our help she stands a chance . . . maybe for the first time.

It's not that I'm naive or a pie-in-the-sky optimist. I just have a lot of faith in God. I know He can really help our kids.

And day by day, kid by kid, I've seen what the staff and volunteers of Covenant House can do . . . .

There's something truly mysterious about the Covenant we make with our kids. When a kid comes to our doors, the first thing we do is tell him how glad we are he came to us and tell him something he has probably never heard before—"we believe in you. We trust you. We're going to do all we can to help you. All we ask is that you do all you can to help yourself."

Most of our kids have never heard such beautiful words in their life . . . . It takes a while before they can believe the words . . . believe in themselves.

I've seen our Covenant work for Jamail, a homeless boy from an abusive home, who proudly walked me through his daily schedule at Covenant House. Jamail is one of our newer kids, having only been with us eleven days.

But to him, they may have been the most important eleven days of his life . . . . "Thank you, Sister. Thank you. I've been here eleven days, and I haven't taken no drugs. I'm so proud of myself . . . Covenant House really helped me."

The covenant—I've seen it work for hundreds of our kids, in a million different ways. I think I could spend five books telling you what it means to them. But I think one of our kids said it best to a television reporter. A feature was being prepared, and the reporter asked if it would be alright to interview some of the kids. We stepped out into the hallway and began talking to the first kid who happened along, a beautiful young girl with a darling baby on her hip. The baby looked precious with little ribbons in her hair.

This young lady had come to us strung out on drugs and five months pregnant. Now she was back on her feet.

"What has Covenant House done for you?" the reporter asked.

"Covenant House has taught me to be responsible for myself, and to do the things that are good for me. It's taught me that I am somebody."

Kids like this teach me a lot, too . . . .

HOW TO TALK TO YOUR TEEN

Listen, really listen. Don't try to listen while doing something else. Put your chores aside so your teen knows you're really paying attention.

Tolerate differences. View your teenager as an individual distinct from you. But this doesn't mean you can't state your opinion if you disagree.

Never imply that your teenager's feelings don't matter or that they will change. Teens live in the present. It doesn't help them to know they'll soon feel differently.

Chapter 3
Michael

Last night Michael had been a success story . . . and now he had slit his wrists.

Last night, Michael had stood before an audience of 32 street kids and told them about his life . . . "My name is Michael, and I'm a recovering drug addict."

Michael has a baby face and a smile full of bright white teeth. He's the kind of kid you trust at first sight. But in reality, his deep brown eyes hid a lot of pain.

When he first arrived at Covenant House, Michael had an attitude that wouldn't quit. He constantly harassed the counselors, threatening to "report" them if they disagreed with him. He refused to admit that he had any problems—especially not with drugs. Finally Frankie, one of our best counselors, stood up to him. "Well then, what are you doing here?" she demanded.

Michael stood dumbfounded for a minute, and then tears began to flow. "Because I have no place else to go," he said. "Covenant House is my only hope, the only place I'm wanted . . . and safe. Now I've probably screwed that up, too."

When he was 15, Michael told his mother and stepfather that he was homosexual. His stepfather couldn't handle it and kicked him out of the house—but Michael had nowhere to go. So he ended up on the streets of New York, where the dealers and the sex industry swallowed him up. When he first came to Covenant House, he was a desperate drug addict who supported himself and his habit by selling his body on the streets.

But Michael was no different than countless other homeless kids caught in the web of street life—having to do awful things just to survive.

When he found out that Covenant House might be able to help him escape from the street, he struggled to break the ties with his past and come to us.

Frankie convinced Michael to enter our drug abuse program. A year later, clean at last at age 20, Michael was speaking in front of the Covenant House kids. "I'll be leaving tomorrow," he said. "Thanks to Covenant House, I've found a great job with a law firm. I'll miss everyone here, and I'll never forget you." He turned his gaze to the counselors, standing proudly at the back of the room.

Then, turning to the kids, his voice broke as he said, "Please, the people here at Covenant House will always reach out a hand to help you . . . grab it! And don't look back." When Michael had finished speaking, all the kids gathered around him for a group hug that lasted about five minutes. All total strangers, all scared, in trouble, all just children.

Then a little later that night, Michael slit both his wrists.

Thank God we found him in the morning. "I didn't want to let you down," he said, through rivers of tears at the hospital. "Suddenly it was all so real, and I didn't think I could go through with it. I didn't want to disappoint you."

If only he could understand that nothing could sadden and disappoint us as much as los-

ing him. He was right on the brink of everything good in life . . . but his life on the streets
had made him believe that he didn't deserve it,
that he couldn't do it. And after all our work
together, we were back to square one, it
seemed. The only thing that helps me go on in
situations like this is that I'm constantly
amazed by the boundless love people are capable of showing each other when the hour is
darkest.

We brought Michael back to Covenant
House when he was released from the hospital
and he had the courage to start again with the
painful process of putting his life back together. Then one day, he came to Frankie and
said, "I want to find my father. Not my mother's husband—my real father."

"Michael," Frankie told him, "your father
may not want to see you. It's been a long time."
We all felt Michael was setting himself up for a
huge disappointment. We assumed that even if
he could find his father, he wouldn't want his
son back. Why should he want a son he didn't
know—a son with problems so big that he'd
slashed his own wrists?

So many of these kids don't know their fa-
thers . . . .And it takes on such a great impor-

tance to them to find out who that man is. Michael was one of those who wouldn't be satisfied until he found his father. We had to help him try.

And this explains what I mean about being amazed by the love and understanding that God built into these fragile hearts of ours. Michael's father was overjoyed to hear from his son, problems and all! In fact, he invited Michael to come and live with him, and we had the happy privilege of sending him off to California to be with his dad. Not long afterward, Michael called to let us know he was working; he was still off drugs, and he was enrolled in college beginning in the Fall. I've been thanking God a lot for letting us help Michael!

Michael had a lot of problems in his young life . . . . And probably the worst one was drug addiction. Almost all of the kids we see have taken drugs, and some of them are addicts. I know about drugs. I know what they do to children. When I was assigned to help found the Bushwick Human Services Center in Brooklyn, I began an education that taught me more than years of graduate school ever did. I learned straight away that drugs are rampant. They are everywhere. They are the single biggest threat to these kids . . . poor kids trying to escape the pain of a life where nobody wants them . . . trying to forget that their families won't or just can't care for them.

Once I asked a group of kids at Covenant House how far they would have to be from the Center to buy drugs. "You might get to the corner," they said . . . about 40 yards from our door.

Why is the temptation of drugs so great for these kids? I saw again, just the other day, just how powerful the pull is. I was standing on a street corner, waiting for the light to change, when a beautiful black Porsche pulled up to the curb. The paint was immaculate, the hubcaps were shiny gold, the dashboard looked like a NASA command post. I was so surprised to see that Jason, a kid who used to be in one of my classes, was the driver. He must be about 20 years old now, and it was obvious he had to be dealing drugs to afford a car like that. I talked to him for a minute there at the side of the street, and he seemed to be pretty embarrassed. "I'm going to have a talk with your mother, Jason," I told him. "I'm worried about you."

I'd always been welcome in their home, and his mother let me in, but she seemed upset that I was there. I told her I was afraid that Jason was up to bad things and might get hurt. Finally his mom stood and went to the corner of her kitchen where there was a brand new refrigerator. "Sister," she said, "I never had one of these in my whole life. Now I do."

I looked at her and tried to tell her how badly I felt, how worried I was about her child, how wrong I thought she was . . . but the words just wouldn't come out. How do you tell a 46-year-old woman living in the ghetto who just got her very first refrigerator, that she should give it back? How?

The vicious cycle of poverty, drugs, crime lives in the ghetto with more powerful chains than a prison . . . locking in kids with little hope.

At Covenant House, when a kid comes to us with a drug problem, we're there to help. We have sponsored thousands of youngsters through drug treatment programs, and we're justly proud of our successes.

We're very proud of the next kid I want to meet, a wonderful kid named Jimmy. . . .

WHAT TO DO IF YOU THINK YOUR TEEN IS USING DRUGS

First, you must understand the four levels of drug use: experimentation, controlled use, abuse, and dependence—and then react accordingly.

Experimentation. If your child is just starting to try drugs, the worst thing you could do is accuse him of being a "drug fiend." Overreaction can actually make the child use drugs more—in rebellion.

Instead, be subtle. Quietly tell him you feel he may be getting into something dangerous. Don't accuse or lecture. Ask why he wants to try drugs, and explain that you don't want drugs to interfere with his health and his goals in life.

Controlled use refers to the occasional drug user. In this case, the person does not allow the drug to control him, or interfere with his work. Again, in this situation, it is best to approach your child gently with your concerns, without overreacting.

Abuse. People cross the line from controlled use to abuse when they start using drugs frequently and excessively. If you're convinced your child is an abuser, tell him you love him and want to help him with his problem. If he doesn't stop, convince him to go to a counselor with you.

Dependence occurs when the drug controls the person. In this case, the user is self-destructive and you must act decisively and forcefully. Carry your child to a treatment center if you have to.

Chapter 4
Jimmy

"Please let us in. Some guy just tried to pick me up. Take us with you. Please don't break up our family. We want to stay with each other."

It was 2:30 in the morning, in one of the roughest neighborhoods in the city. Fifteen-year-old Jimmy and his little "family," his sister and half-sister, stood outside our Covenant House van, fear written all over their faces.

It was only their first or second night alone—homeless—on the street.

Jimmy's dad had killed himself. Their mom was somewhere, they didn't know where, dying of AIDS. Everything they had in the world was scrunched inside a big green plastic bag Jimmy had flung over his shoulder.

Please . . . please read on and let me tell you what happened to these youngsters. Because

something just like it is happening again tonight . . . right now.

You see, as you go to sleep tonight, thousands of homeless boys and girls like Jimmy
will be out on America's city streets . . . alone
. . . terrified . . . .

These young people are the most under-
privileged, underloved segment in all of American society. While most youngsters their age
are safely tucked away in bed at night, children
like Jimmy wander the streets in the dark. The
bruises on their faces don't show under neon
lights. You can't see their pain and tears in
night's shadows.

For eight hours each night, from 10:00 PM
till 6:00 AM, Covenant House's vans plunge
into the night and the horror of high-risk city
areas, reaching out to lost and homeless street
kids. It's our job to find them . . . and try our
best to help them.

Our van staff is specially trained to dis-
pense hope . . . and a generous helping of
hearty sandwiches and lemonade. It's dangerous work. The vans have been shot at. Wher-
ever kids are on the street, there's sometimes a
pimp in the shadows. Pimps know about our
vans, and they don't like them. Occasionally

we talk a kid into getting in. The pimp loses money-making "property" and part of his reputation for being able to protect his "own."

So kids—especially the girls—who come up to the van get punished. We think that's what happened to a girl who came to get lemonade a couple of weeks ago. Anyway, we never saw her again. Maybe she was punished. Or worse . . . .

But some brave kids get into the van and come back with us to Covenant House. Others sip their drinks for a few minutes and talk to us. Every night, a few voices speak out of the shadows . . . .

"Jump in," I said, "You guys must be really tired. Would you like some sandwiches and lemonade?"

Jimmy and his sisters dove into the sandwiches as our van whisked them back to our crisis shelter. Their story was pretty typical . . . it really hurt to hear it.

Jimmy's father had committed suicide when Jimmy was two years old, right after his youngest sister was born. Their mother had tried to raise the kids, but she couldn't cope. After years of poverty and despair, she sunk into the world of drugs and prostitution.

Then, one day recently, she learned she was dying of AIDS. So she packed up her things, what little she had, and vanished into the night.

We drove Jimmy and his little family back to Covenant House and got them inside. They felt safe when they saw the guys at the door. (God has sent a few of his biggest servants to Covenant House to help protect the kids. Pimps used to try to break in and get their girls back.)

The next day we took them to a group home. We're trying to find a real family for them to live with. One thing Jimmy insists on—that they stay together. "We're all we've got." But that's a lot more than most homeless kids have.

I wish you could spend just one night in one of our vans. I wish you could see how you can penetrate the darkness and call out to the innocence and the beauty of these kids.

Kids like Jimmy are good kids. You'd see God's face behind the horror. I know you would.

And you'd see a lot—I mean a lot—of these faces out on our vans. I think these statistics will show you why:

* Every 8 seconds of every school day, a child drops out of school.
* Every 26 seconds a child runs away from home.
* Every 47 seconds a child is seriously abused or neglected.
* Every 67 seconds a teenager has a baby.
* Every 7 minutes a child is arrested for drug abuse.
* Every 36 minutes a child is killed or injured by a gun.
* Every day, 135,000 American children carry their guns with them to school.

We hear a lot of talk about providing a "safety net" for the poor. How I wish we weren't the only safety net for these kids.

Covenant House is here to catch these kids and do all we can. It's just too bad our hands are so busy. Some of the kids—too many of the kids—just drop through.

HOW TO BE YOUR TEEN'S BEST FRIEND

Set aside some quality time to share with your teen on a regular basis.

Find some activity you can enjoy together. It can be as simple as taking a walk, going to a show or the movies, or perhaps just going to a restaurant together.

Be honest with your teen. When you're angry or disappointed, explain why. When you're happy, share your joy. Give praise and encouragement when you're pleased with your teen's behavior or accomplishments.

Be a good listener.

Trust your teen to "do the right thing" after you've offered your advice and guidance.

Forgive and forget. Everybody makes mistakes. Allow your teen to learn from them.

Say "I love you."

Chapter 5
Wendy

"Um . . . excuse me . . . can I talk to you for a minute?"

She stood at the front of the chapel after Mass, shifting her weight from one foot to the other, her eyes filled with tears.

Her name was Wendy, a pretty 18-year-old girl with black hair, translucent skin, and high cheekbones that gave her the look of a model. She might have been one in another, different lifetime.

But Wendy's life didn't work out that way . . . .

"I just wanted to tell you something. I just wanted to say thank you for taking in kids like me. I don't . . . I don't know where I'd be if I hadn't come here."

"Julie wants to thank you, too."

She beamed at the child she had in her arms. I'll never forget that look on her face . . . she was so proud and happy for her little five-month-old. Julie cooed a few baby sounds, then let out a little giggle. I'm sure God broke into a big smile, too.

I know God has spent a lot of time looking after Wendy these last few months.

You see, Wendy is what our society cruelly refers to as a "systems kid" . . . a kid without a family. Since she was given up at two years old, she'd lived in 12 foster homes.

Then one day Wendy did something little kids in "the system" aren't supposed to do—she turned eighteen.

Suddenly, overnight, Wendy didn't have a place in the world to go. As she told us . . . .

"That's when things started getting really bad. I had to leave, but I didn't know anybody. I didn't know where to go. I felt like nobody wanted me."

"So I just headed for the city. I thought I could get a job there. But getting an apartment was so expensive! I got a job . . . but I couldn't pay the rent. After a few months, I was thrown out . . . I ended up on the streets without any place to go."

"I met a man, and he said he'd help me. But . . . well . . . he made me take drugs with him, and do some awful stuff. He got me pregnant. It was really terrible. I just ran away one day. . . I couldn't take it anymore."

That was six months ago, when Wendy ended up at Covenant House. She was homeless . . . totally alone . . . and eight months pregnant.

I thank God that Wendy ended up on our doorstep! And we were able to make sure her baby was born safely. . . healthy. . . alive.

Today? Wendy's a lot better. She's graduated from our drug abuse program with flying colors. And we've been able to find her a job, and a nice place for her and the baby to live.

It was a really nice moment in the chapel with Wendy. . . kind of a baptism. *A new life!* A little girl who was lost when she came to Covenant House six months earlier had now found herself. A tiny infant whose future seemed hopeless six months ago, was now riding alongside a loving mother, flying on the very wings of hope.

Thanks to our special programs for homeless pregnant teenagers, a lot of girls like Wendy—kids with kids who otherwise wouldn't have a prayer in the world—are making two lives better. I think this letter I got recently from one of our Covenant House kids says it better than I ever could. Her name is Cathy, and her short letter was one of the most beautiful things I've ever read. I hope you enjoy it, too . . . .

Dear Staff,

My name is Cathy. I was a resident at the Covenant House off and on all of last year.

The purpose of this letter is to thank all of you for being there for me. I have no idea where I would be today if the Covenant House didn't exist. Well actually I do know, I'd be dead.

Being out in the streets was a living hell for me. It seemed like two lifetimes.

Within these past few months, I've been thinking of how grateful I am for all of the things you've done for me, the clothing on my back, the roof over my head, and the food in my stomach.

I was and always will be grateful for the Covenant House.

As of today, I'm living a clean and sober life. I will be attending school in September for Human Services and hope to work with homeless teenagers.

My long term goal in life is to have a shelter of my own.

It's such a huge problem today and so much needs to be done about it.

There is so much I need to address to all of you. The bottom line is this, I'd like to say THANK YOU SO MUCH AND I LOVE YOU ALL!!!

Love always,

Cathy

P.S. My prayers are with everyone there.

SOME HELPFUL READING

If you know a parent of a teenager who needs extra help, you may want to recommend these books (of course, our NINELINE counselors are always ready to help, and just a free phone call away—1-800-999-9999).

Buntman, Peter H., M.S.W., ACSW, and Eleanor M. Saris, M. Ed. *How to Live With Your Teenager: A Survivor's Handbook for Parents*, (New York: Ballantine, 1979).

Ginott, Dr. Haim G. *Between Parent and Teenager* (New York: Avon Books, 1971).

Kolodny, Dr. Robert C. and Nancy, and Dr. Thomas E. Bratter and Cheryl Deep. *How to Survive Your Adolescent's Adolescence* (Boston: Little & Brown, 1984).

Smith, Manual J., Ph.D. *Yes, I Can Say No: A Parent's Guide to Assertiveness Training for Children* (New York: Arbor House, 1986).

Youngs, Bettie B. *Helping Your Teenager Deal with Stress: A Parent's Survival Guide* (Los Angeles: Jeremy Tarcher, 1986).

Chapter 6
Clarissa

"Thank you," she said, handing me a box wrapped in paper. "Thank you for being an influence in our lives."

"Yes, thank you," he stammered.

They stood before me with tears in their eyes. Her name was Clarissa, President of the Resident's Council in our Rights of Passage program. His name was Eric, the Council's Vice-President. One year ago, these kids had something else in common besides a yearning for leadership. One year ago they were two homeless kids.

I took the present and unwrapped it carefully. Then I swallowed hard and struggled to keep my tears inside. It was a beautiful glass paperweight with our Covenant House symbol inside.

I like the name of our Rights of Passage program, I thought, looking at the image poised inside the fragile glass globe: a dove supported by a helping hand, the symbol of Covenant House—but I love what it does: helps kids reclaim their right to the future.

Clarissa and Eric aren't exactly the type of kids who would have been elected to the Student Council in their old high schools.

For starters, half the time they wouldn't even have been in class. Eric was spending more and more of his time on the street, getting into the kind of trouble that had him headed straight to jail or an early grave; and Clarissa, homeless at 17, had made the mistake of "looking for love in all the wrong places," and gotten pregnant. So at 17 and 18, instead of looking forward to the future with the kind of hope and dreams all kids their age should have, they were already sad failures in their own eyes, well on their way to being just two more tragic statistics.

And in 1990, the statistics were especially bleak for children like Eric and Clarissa struggling to grow up:

* 55% of teenagers living in single-parent households live at the poverty level.
* The number of teen suicides has doubled since 1970.
* The school dropout rate is as high as 60% in many major U.S. cities.
* The number of 15-year-old girls who are sexually active has doubled since 1990.
* 10% of girls, ages 15 to 19, get pregnant every year.
* 60% of all high school seniors say they have drunk alcohol in the past 30 days.

Statistics like these make me heartsick; worse, they can tempt you to lose hope, and hope is hard to hold onto. It's like a wounded bird that hops into your hand. You don't know if the poor creature is going to get frightened and fly away before you have a chance to reach out and help it.

I picked up the paperweight and held it in my hands. Why didn't Clarissa fly away, I wondered? What did we do that made her stay? And then I remembered the testimony she gave at our annual dinner last year . . . the testimony so many people have told me about.

She stood there at the podium nervously, facing hundreds and hundreds of people gathered in the elegant ballroom of the Waldorf Astoria Hotel in New York.

It was an emotional story, of how she had moved from a broken home to a new life of dignity and meaning after she found Covenant House. "I needed to find a job, and through the Educational/Vocational Department here, I've obtained a great job with a prestigious advertising agency," she said. "I also use the Infant-/Toddler Center. During my work hours, my son is cared for by the day-care staff. And in the evenings, the staff meets with mothers and we discuss parenting issues. I've learned a lot about raising my son from these sessions. And I've been able to exercise my management and organization skills on the Resident Council. I believe in getting involved, and it feels good to have residents as well as staff believe in me."

Then she hesitated. There was so much more she wanted to say, but it was hard to put into words.

"Here at Rights of Passage," the young woman said, her voice wavering, "I'm encouraged to be myself, and to reach for the goals I have set for myself and my child . . . . When I first came into the program, what I expected was to be given the time and freedom to get my life together. What I didn't expect is what makes the program so special . . . ."

And then she stopped and looked at the sea of attentive faces looking back at her with genuine love and concern . . . and enormous pride. "Having a mentor is another great part of the program. With my volunteer mentor, I have the opportunity to work with someone whom I can look up to and learn from. And for the first time in my life," she said, her voice barely above a whisper now—but a whisper you could hear clear up to the crystal chandeliers—"I experienced uncondi . . . ." And here she had to stop altogether, because she began to cry.

She was so embarrassed: There she was, standing in front of hundreds of people, and she couldn't finish.

Unconditional love, she wanted to say, but she couldn't get the words out. It didn't matter: Thunderous applause from the audience finished her story.

Bruce Henry, our program's director, reports that 20% of our Rights of Passage graduates go on to college, and that 70% of them get employment earning $7 an hour or more.

Pretty good for kids who had no chance, no choices not too long ago.

HOW TO SPEAK UP WHEN GRADES GO DOWN

Deteriorating performance in school is a problem that most parents must deal with at one point or another. Here are some tips that will help:

- **Be a friend, not an adversary.** Let your child know that you realize how hard it is to do well in school— and be ready to help. Teach him better study habits. Pump up her self-esteem. And have him tested if you suspect there may be a learning disability.

- **Look for the underlying reasons** for the poor performance. Rather than just scolding or punishing your child, try to find out *why* she's having trouble at school. Is there friction in the household? Does your child feel excluded from the social scene at school? Has he experienced the loss of a friend or relative?

- **Be realistic about your kid's capabilities.** One of the worst things a parent can do is demand more of a child than he is capable of. Not all kids can become doctors, lawyers or scientists. Perhaps she has a talent for art, music, athletics, or working with tools. Encourage your child's strengths while helping to work on the weaknesses.

Chapter 7
Michelle

"My mother hates me," Michelle told me with a big sigh. I will never get used to hearing that from a child. And I've heard it all too often.

"She even pushed me down the stairs one time, and I was in the hospital for a week. Whenever she couldn't stand me anymore, she'd send me to my dad's house, which I hated because of the things he did to me. So then I'd beg to go back to my mom's house. I must have gone back and forth twenty times."

Sometimes I catch myself thinking that physical and sexual abuse and rejection must harden kids like Michelle. It doesn't. If anything, it makes them more vulnerable than most kids. Some of them pretend they're tough. "After what I've been through, I can handle anything," they'll tell you. But I know the truth. I've walked among the kids at Cove-

nant House at night. I've heard the sniffles and
the sobs. I've learned to recognize the puffy
eyes and dark circles that give away the kids
who cried all night. Sometimes I feel that God
created the dark of night so kids can cry unno-
ticed. The crying eases their pain.

But Michelle was too naive even to pretend
to be tough. "I always just wanted people to
like me," she told me. When she said that, I
winced. I hope she didn't see it. I winced because I know how easily a pimp would trap her
if she was on the streets . . . and what he'd do to
her.

When Michelle finally couldn't stand it at
home anymore, she was placed in foster care.
When she "aged" out of the system in her
home state of Florida, she went to New York
. . . where she found herself at the Port Authority with no money, no home, no one in the
world who cared—or even knew—where she
was. How she escaped the pimps on the prowl,
I'll never know. Maybe she was too naive to
have been scared—pimps look for girls who
are scared. They pretend to be a friend and of-
fer the girls a place to stay. . . .

They could earn academy awards for the
way they play the savior act. But, they deserve

something else for the way they get these children addicted to drugs and then peddle their bodies and souls on the streets. When Michelle got hungry enough and scared enough, she would have been easy prey for them. Luckily, she found her way to Covenant House before the pimps found her.

"God must have been watching out for you," I told her. "He loves you, you know."

"If He loves me, why didn't He answer my prayers and make my mother love me—and my father leave me alone?" Michelle asked.

I never know what to say to that one. I know God loves Michelle; what I can't understand is why her parents hurt her. She is sweet and eager to please with bright blue eyes, curly brown hair, and a face any mother could love.

Michelle is doing well here, and she has earned a place in our long-term Rights of Passage program for older teens. She has an excellent volunteer mentor who is helping her plan her future, and right now she's working in a restaurant and trying to decide about going to school. She doesn't quite believe that God loves her yet, but she believes that we do, and that's a start.

Young girls like Michelle show up at the Port Authority in New York City every day. Many are fleeing abusive homes; many have never known any love.

I'm thinking now of a girl named Christy in our Ft. Lauderdale program. I first saw her at a little prayer group that the kids have organized for themselves. (That's an unbelievable experience in itself—every morning, about twenty of our homeless, hurting kids voluntarily gather in chapel to sing and pray for each other. It was all the kids' idea; they organized it, and it's very, very beautiful.)

When I first saw Christy, she was dressed in a beautiful red dress, sitting poised and polished at a celebration, looking like a million bucks and talking cheerfully with the other kids in the meeting. But, the very next day at the prayer meeting, Christy was down-hearted and sad, "Please pray for my sister," she stammered. "Today's her 16th birthday. And if you don't mind, could you also pray for me? I'm having a really bad day."

That's all she said. Nobody pressed her for details. They didn't need to; they knew what bad days were like. They'd had plenty themselves. And they knew how to pray about it. After the meeting, I invited Christy to come and talk with me. As we walked along together, she started telling me the rest of the story—the part she didn't share with the other kids.

"I called my sister to wish her a happy birthday, then I asked if I could talk to my mom. I hadn't talked with her in three months." Christy paused, took a deep breath, and continued haltingly. "She . . . she got on the phone, and I asked her how she was, and she said, 'I'm much happier now that you're out of my life'."

Can you imagine that? Can you imagine what it must be like to be homeless, to call your own mother, and hear her say, "I'm much happier now that you're out of my life"? I can't even comprehend how that must feel. It just isn't right! Christy might have been a handful when she lived at home, but I could tell just talking with her that she really is a good kid. Like all of our kids, she just needs love and respect . . . and a skillful counselor to help her sort out her problems.

"I guess I was tough to live with," Christy said. "My stepfather, he . . . he used to beat me. I started taking drugs and got really out of control, I guess. One day my mom just threw me out of the house. I ended up on the street. Totally alone. I was really scared. I went to live with three other kids. I really didn't know them very well."

Christy took a deep breath, and settled into a chair. Her long hair fell like strands of silk on her slender shoulders. Her blue jeans, pale green sweatshirt that matched her eyes, and worn tennis shoes were in stark contrast to the lovely outfit I had first seen her in. Now, just a day later, she looked completely different, and much sadder. She put her head back on the soft cushion and looked at the ceiling—maybe hoping God was up there listening to her, too.

"One day my friends moved out. I didn't have a job or anything, so I couldn't pay the rent. The landlord started threatening me and one day I came home and found all my stuff piled outside the door...and the lock was changed."

That's when Christy started living on the street. She sank deeply into drug abuse, and like so many other girls in her situation, she was forced into prostitution to support herself.

"The important thing is that you're here now, Christy," I told her. "You're going to make it. I know you are." I believe that Christy will succeed—because she wants to live a better life. She's trying so hard.

That's what's so constantly amazing about the kids who come through our doors at Covenant House. No matter how battered they've been, no matter how bruised, abused or neglected, they still keep going. They know their life could be better, and they're willing to fight for it. In many ways, they are like the dove which is our symbol—a delicate and fragile bird flying alone, needing the hand below it for help and support.

And, tragically, when these kids come to us, they receive this kind of unconditional love and support for the first time in their lives. They are all too often the victims of parents who didn't or couldn't care for them and quite simply do not want them.

That these kids still keep going is inspiring! In my book, that makes a kid brave. In my book, that makes a kid strong. In my book, that makes a kid proud.

IF YOU ARE A PARENT STRUGGLING WITH A TROUBLED CHILD, REMEMBER . . . .

- Parents are people too.
- Parents' material and emotional resources are limited.
- Blaming keeps people helpless.
- Kids' behavior affects parents.
- Parents' behavior affects kids.
- Taking a stand precipitates a crisis.
- From controlled crisis comes positive change.
- Families need to give and get support in their own community in order to change.

Chapter 8

Kareem

"Hey, do I need a legal permit to have a parade?"

He stood in our lawyer Jay's office—Kareem, five-feet-seven, decked out in his Day-Glo T-shirt and mischievous grin.

"Kareem," Jay asked cautiously, "why do you want to know?"

"I'm gonna get a parade together," Kareem answered. His grin turned into a scowl. "Nobody's payin' attention to us, man! Us street kids need to have our own voice. We need—and we want—to be heard."

There was no use trying to talk Kareem out of it. No use telling him that a five-foot-seven-inch street kid wasn't big enough to do it. You see, Kareem thinks the world of Covenant House. And slick as a professional advance man, he rounded up 74 other kids who do, too.

They had big plans. "Parade permit? Piece of cake!" Kareem laughed. "Make banners? No sweat." And for this kid with the bounce of a Jack-out-of-the-box, it seemed easy.

He got his permit, and he had his parade—the brightest, loudest, most joyous group of rag-tag kids and rainbow-hued banners that ever marched up Broadway. Banners flying, Kareem and his band of street crusaders marched up to Trump Plaza, dug their feet in the pavement and shouted loud enough for God to hear: "Covenant House ain't no dump! We need your help, Donald Trump!"

I don't know if Mr. Trump heard Kareem and the other kids, but they didn't wait around to see. The parade moved on uptown to Gracie Mansion (the Mayor's residence) where—after a lot of chanting—an assistant to the Mayor came out and listened politely while Kareem pleaded his case.

The media had heard about the parade, and they came to hear what the kids had to say. When a reporter asked Kareem why he had organized this demonstration, he said, "If it weren't for Covenant House, I wouldn't have had anywhere else to go."

You would have had a lump in your throat if you'd seen it—our kids marching because they wanted to do something for the place that had done so much for them.

It was especially great to see the determination in Kareem's eyes, the life and the vitality. Because things haven't been easy for this kid. He never knew his mom or dad. He was raised by his grandmother, who really loved him. "She made me feel good, like I wasn't missing anything. And she was a great cook."

But when she died, Kareem wanted to die, too. He came to New York to climb the biggest bridge he could find—and jump off of it. A cab driver prevented Kareem's suicide. He told the boy he'd hold up traffic if he jumped. Today Kareem says, "I cussed him out, but now I'd like to say thanks, cabbie."

Kareem says, "I wandered around for a few days, sleeping on the streets, scrounging some food. Then a kid told me about Covenant House, that they'd give me some food and a bed, so I came."

One morning he slit his wrists in one of our bathrooms.

We had to send him away for a while then, but he bounced right back and returned to us.

And since that time, it's Kareem's antics that have us bouncing off the walls. His latest caper even saved a little boy from being kidnapped!

"Me and my man Johnny, we was walking by the Port Authority, and we saw this sad-looking black kid, looked ten years old. This older woman was standing next to him, smokin' crack. But the kid was dressed in middle-class clothes, not like a street chicken."

(A "chicken" is a street term for a youngster who is a target for sexual abuse.)

"I sensed bad vibes, man. I went up with Johnny to this kid and asked him, 'You alright?' This crack-smokin' chick growls at us, 'This is my kid. Get lost.' Then these two big dudes come over and say, 'Beat it!' Like a blur, me and Johnny grab the kid, and we zig-zag like Michael Jordan past pimps, whores, chickens, coke and crackheads, and hustle the kid into Covenant House."

The little boy had been kidnapped shortly before! Kareem and Johnny rescued him, and the New York District Attorney thanked them for their bravery. When the little boy's mother offered to reward them, Kareem asked her to give the money to Covenant House instead.

All this happens in just a few short months in the life of a kid at Covenant House. One day he's trying to commit suicide; then he's trying to plead our case in front of the Mayor of New York; then he's rescuing another kid from life on the streets. That's why we always find room for every kid who comes to Covenant House . . . because every kid deserves this chance.

When the Good Samaritan passed the injured man on the road, he didn't need his life story to decide whether or not the poor man was worth his trouble . . . . He just leaned over and picked the dying man up off the street.

When Kareem came to Covenant House, he was looking for more than food and shelter— he was looking for a reason to live, and he found it. But not without a struggle. Now that he knows how good it feels to help somebody else, he's found a reason to live. The other day he told us he wants to become a cab driver. "Maybe I can keep some other kid from jumpin' off a bridge." Too many of our kids need somebody to keep them from jumping off a bridge today.

I'm always so proud of kids like Kareem. The minute they get back on their feet, they immediately think of the other kids out there on the street, the kids still left behind. I hope Kareem does end up driving a cab if that's what he wants to do—because in the "never-too-strange-to-believe world" of our Covenant House kids, cab drivers seem to be saving lives left and right!

Take the bizarre story of Joey, a kid we met just last week. Joey was one of those kids who appeared to have the "ideal" life. He lived in a big house on a beautiful tree-lined street in the suburbs. Went to all the best schools. Got all the best marks. Was raised by a mother and father who were pillars of their community.

Except one thing was missing from Joey's life—the feeling of truly being loved. According to Joey, "My parents never bothered to talk to me . . . even when I got all A's in school, it never seemed enough." So one day in anger and desperation he went to the bank down the street, took out every penny of his life savings, and went to the airport asking for a flight "to the most far away place I can go without a passport." Twelve hours later, Joey landed in Anchorage, Alaska, completely alone, and only a few dollars in his pocket.

Fortunately, one of America's cab drivers came to the rescue again. As soon as Joey hailed a cab at the airport, he asked to go to someplace where he could get help . . . where people cared about him. The cab driver took him to our Covenant House in Anchorage. Within three hours, Joey was on the phone with his distraught parents, and back on his way home, where he is now safe and sound.

I tell you this story because it not only shows kids can end up anywhere (who would have thought a runaway would choose to go to Alaska!), but they come from everywhere, too. From the best homes, in the best suburbs. And no method of "escape" is too bizarre or out of the question . . . whether you're talking about a kid taking a long plane ride, or a long jump off a bridge.

But, we're grateful for Joey. He is one of our very rare "easy" cases. We got to him before the ravages of the street could. And he had a home to go back to . . . parents who loved him and wanted to do better.

When I think about kids like Kareem, who has already tried to commit suicide twice, and Joey, who seemed to have the world at his fingertips and instead chose to escape to another world 3,000 miles away, I'm reminded of the analogy that our lives are like a tapestry. If you look at the back of a tapestry, what do you see? A lot of knots and threads, some loose ends, some broken off and retied . . . . The back of a tapestry is just a mess of colored threads.

Yet when you turn that mess over, you see a stunning pattern and design—and the connection between the two sides is almost unrecognizable. God is the weaver who pulls the threads in the tapestries of our lives. When you look at a life like Kareem's, on the back side you see the jumble of knots—the suicide attempts, the depression, the highs and lows. But on the flip side, you see a brilliant design, you find the beauty in each kid. You discover Kareem is a hero, saving other kids from life on the streets . . . . And you thank God that the few kids like Joey who have a home, actually get back there safely.

HOW WELL DO YOU KNOW YOUR KIDS?

You may say, "My teenager wouldn't do that." Most don't. But even if yours wouldn't, think about the following questions:

- Where is your child right now?
- What are your teen's deepest fears?
- Who is your son's or daughter's best friend?
- Do your teen's friends feel welcome in your home?

Remember, a strong relationship with your children is the best way for you to guide them, and to prevent them from becoming a sorry statistic.

Chapter 9
Ellen

If I'm not talking about it, I'm thinking about it: that "magic moment" in our work when one person's heart touches another's. You really can't measure it, you sure can't put a price on it, but it's worth everything in the world at a place like Covenant House.

I was sitting at my desk just this morning when the phone rang and interrupted my thoughts.

"Sister," Mattie said, her voice sounding urgent, "can you get down here right away? I have something real important to show you."

When a counselor at Covenant House tells you that, you don't waste any time. You know it has to be important.

I was a little out of breath by the time I got to the center, but Mattie wasn't in her office. She told me once that she only spends time there when she's talking heart to heart with a kid and they have something really important to tell her. "Over here, Sister," Mattie called, waving at me from our lounge, where kids congregate between meals and appointments with counselors. She had a triumphant smile on her face. "That's Ellen," she said, pointing out a young girl seated in the midst of a bunch of kids, laughing and talking and waiting for lunch.

"Can't be," I said, taking a step closer. "That can't be Ellen." I didn't want to stare, but it was almost impossible not to.

"Remember the day she came in?" Mattie asked. She didn't have to remind me. Ellen was one of the saddest kids we had seen in a long time.

Mattie remembers talking to her—at least, trying to that first day. "She was like a cat backed into a corner, cursing and spitting and putting its claws out. 'I don't need you,' she kept saying, 'I don't have a problem. I can stop drugs any time.'" "Wow," Mattie said, glancing over at her again, "that child was so messed up, so sick, and bleeding, too."

She was so skinny. A dirty rag was wrapped around her head and she had dry, ashy skin, too—one of the telltale signs of crack abuse.

But Ellen wasn't just a teenage crack user. "I didn't always live like this," she said to me, mumbling under her breath, seeming ashamed of the way she looked. When she was 13, she lived in a nice apartment in New York City with her mother and father. "A nice place," she told me, tears in her eyes, "with plants and sunshine and my own bed, too." But then tragedy struck—her mother died of cancer—and struck again: her father, grief-stricken, had a stroke and died, too.

Terrified at the thought of becoming somebody else's foster child, Ellen decided to try it on her own. But, instead of resting her head on a pillow at night, she laid down on a hard concrete sidewalk and home became one of those cardboard boxes you see if you walk outside the doors of Covenant House.

Mattie made sure Ellen got a shower right away and a decent meal. And slept in a bed with a real pillow. "She came in to see me the next day, and already she looked better," Mattie said. "You could tell by the way her skin looked: it was coming back to life."

Mattie's job is really just to meet the kids and find out what they need, but she doesn't let her job end there.

Ellen took one look at Mattie's face and knew she could trust her. "She told me she had a stomach ache," Mattie said. "Turns out she was bleeding from an infection. She had had a prescription from the hospital, but it ran out. A few weeks ago, to make matters worse, Ellen attempted suicide.

Sick with herself, Ellen had started doing crack to take away her shame, and then selling herself to buy more crack. "She was caught in a vicious cycle," Mattie said sympathetically, shaking her head. "It's like digging a hole that you keep falling through, that crack. Kids think they can challenge the street and win. They just don't know, because the street always, always wins out."

Mattie should know. She's been here since we opened our walk-in clinic in Times Square in 1977, a "Mash Unit" that began rescuing sick and dying street kids like Ellen. This gray-haired grandmother has seen it all—"all the awful things that happen to kids out there"—but what gets to her most is the despair that can drive a desperate youngster like Ellen to suicide.

"Now that Ellen's made it this far," Mattie says happily, "the next step is to talk her into sticking around for awhile so we can get her into a substance abuse program. All we have to do is keep her around for a few more weeks until we can find a place for her. Just a few more weeks . . . ." Mattie pleaded. And then she lowered her voice to barely a whisper.

"Sister, I have to tell you, sometimes I wonder how I keep going. But then I see what happens when you give the worst kid the best you've got—and it's like a miracle, seeing them come back to life." She didn't have to say any more. I took one last look at Ellen and mouthed a silent "thank you" to Mattie and a silent one to God, too. Sometimes I wonder what we did to deserve Mattie. She should be home with her own grandchildren instead of being surrogate grandmother to thousands of street kids, but Covenant House is able to work its magic every day because of people like her. And she's not alone, either.

As you read this, there are some 1,500 Covenant House workers—staff and volunteers—working round the clock to help kids like Ellen. And they never get a moment to rest! Last year, we helped 28,000 homeless kids, and spent three times more helping them than the entire federal government.

People like Mattie make it all possible
. . . .

HOW TO TALK TO YOUR TEEN ABOUT SEX

Start by admitting your anxiety. It's natural to be a little nervous. By admitting your feelings, you start the conversation off on a note of honesty and candor.

Don't try to be an expert. You're not supposed to be Masters and Johnson. Talk about your own teenage years —your feelings and experiences—to get your teen talking.

Team up with your spouse. Kids are fascinated by the details of their parents' early romance. Start talking about yourselves casually, and the rest of the discussion will take care of itself.

Don't make agreement your goal. The purpose of any parent-teenager discussion is to share information, ideas and feelings, not to achieve agreement on every issue. Don't pry or accuse.

Teach the difference between love and sex. Too many kids (and adults) confuse sex and love. Tell your kids that sex without love is wrong.

Give them a book you can discuss together. There are lots of good books about sex. Find one you feel comfortable with—make sure it is age-appropriate and reflects your religious and moral convictions. Give it to your teen and talk about it later.

Chapter 10
Robby

"Dying is easy," Robby said once. "Living is tough." Maybe that's true for kids like Robby. He lived the last bit of his sad life at Covenant House. Robby was dying of AIDS.

One of his best friends here was Jay, our lawyer. They met because Robby wanted to make a will.

"I want to leave everything to a friend of mine," he said. But what did he have to leave to his friend? "A stereo and a hundred bucks."

It wasn't much of a legacy, but the real legacy Robby left was for those of us at Covenant House. It is a legacy of bravery and dignity in the face of death, by a boy who should have lived much, much longer.

At the very end, when Robby was hospitalized, Jay would visit him. Despite Jay's best professional manner, he would find himself laughing at Robby's jokes—even when he had prepared himself for the solemnity he thought death deserved.

"Look, Ma, no tubes!" Robby called one day as Jay came into his room. "I'm feeling much better, Jay. The doctor took me off the IV."

How could a youngster suffering such a cruel fate have the courage to laugh as death approached? I admit, the question confuses me, too. But then, most things about Robby were confusing. He was a streetwise kid—just talk to him for two minutes, and you knew that. But at the same time, an incredible sweetness would shine through his cool, hard shell.

Physically beautiful, Robby had thin, distinguished features and blond, blond hair. He also had great style.

Still, Robby was a very mixed-up kid. He had big problems finding his identity and living with his sexuality. Yet no matter how mixed-up he was, we couldn't help admiring Robby, too. I only hope those of us who think we know what life is all about will show a fraction of the courage Robby showed in the face of death.

But that's one thing that our kids with AIDS seem to have in common. Although they ought to be bitter and scared about their impending deaths, they seem to handle their fate much better than we who love them do. For us, each time we visit one of our kids who has made the final leg of the journey to the hospital, we feel like crying. Yet there in the rooms where they'll surely die, those brave youngsters joke and smile—for our sakes. They don't want us to feel bad.

Larry is another kid we lost to AIDS recently. A member of our volunteer family, Lisa, had been visiting him each afternoon, and she was there when he died. Lisa said, "As much as I'd prayed for Larry's release, the reality of it was hard for me to accept—even though I knew Larry would be much better off now. He'd had such a painful life. His parents never loved him. He'd lived on the streets for years, until he finally started turning his life around at Covenant House. There was a glimmer of hope that he would make it. Then he was diagnosed with AIDS."

"He took the news with incredible bravery. I guess Larry had already faced such disappointment and hurt that knowing he was going to die wasn't that traumatic."

There is so much we can do for the Robbys and Larrys who come to Covenant House. We can provide safety, medical care and most important . . . we can give them dignity.

In the end, we love them as they die, we comfort and pray for them. And, they leave us with the inspiration of their brave hearts.

HOW TO WIN YOUR TEEN'S COOPERATION

Always try to understand what your child is feeling.

You don't have to agree or condone to understand. If possible, share an example of a time when you felt the same.

Share your feelings about the situation in a non-accusing manner. Children are willing to hear you after they feel heard.

Work together on ideas to avoid the problem in the future—or to correct the present problem through a logical consequence.

If the first three steps have been done in a respectful manner, your child will be ready for cooperation in the fourth step.

Chapter 11
Amy

"Please help me . . . let me stay here . . . can I stay here, please?"

She came sprinting past the front door, and hurled herself through like a blast of cold air. She was 5 foot 2, with blue eyes and a frail winsome body. She was a little girl with bruises all over her body.

And she was running in her bare feet.

Even though it was cold outside, Amy was running through the cold and snow without shoes.

"I'm sorry . . . I hope I didn't break any rules. The guard looked pretty mad when I didn't stop. But I couldn't stop . . . this guy I know is after me . . . he said he's going to kill me . . . ."

"This guy is really dangerous. *He took away my shoes so I couldn't run.* Please let me stay here . . . please!!!"

She hobbled over to a chair, and sat down, and pulled her knees up. Even from twenty feet away, we could see she was trembling. Then, the dam burst. A stream of tears began to run down her cheeks . . . .

You could have heard a pin drop in our shelter.

One of the counselors sat alongside Amy and told her to take her time. Finally, slowly, her story spilled out . . . .

Amy was from the Midwest. She'd run away from home after her alcoholic stepfather abused her. At the bus station in New York, a man named Tiger befriended her and promised to take care of her. But a few days later he turned on her, beat her into submission, and put her on the street to earn money as a prostitute.

When Amy tried to run away, he threatened to kill her. And then he took away her shoes.

Amy needed some time by herself when she got to Covenant House. She didn't want to be with the other kids. So, we took her up to one of our offices.

She slept that first day, right on the floor. It looked like the first restful sleep she'd had in weeks. The next day, she was back, sleeping on the floor again. The third day, she was coughing uncontrollably.

We took her to the hospital. It was last Christmas Eve. Amy had pneumonia. And she was convinced she had AIDS.

But, this story has a happy ending!

You see, our barefoot runaway is now a walking, talking miracle. She's long since out of the hospital, and has gone through a drug program (her pimp got her hooked on drugs . . . a lot of pimps do that to the girls).

She's also finishing up in school, and will soon have the high school diploma she needs to get a job.

Best of all, Amy doesn't have AIDS! The doctors tested her the day after Christmas last year, and gave her a clean bill of health. You should have seen the smile on her face that morning!

We're so hopeful for Amy—and very proud of her, too.

You know, ever since I came to Covenant House I've been overwhelmed with stories like this. I wanted to share this one with you, because it hit me so hard.

I keep thinking about what it must have been like for Amy in that hospital bed last Christmas...especially the first night. I've been told she didn't speak to anyone...she was too tired to even open her eyes. Maybe she was dreaming about Christmases when she was little, when her mom was still alive and her stepfather hadn't hurt her.

Or maybe she was just wondering how a nice girl ends up all alone in a hospital bed on Christmas Eve, in a big, strange city, with no friends, and aching feet. It must have torn her heart apart that night....

I guess Amy's story might sound almost like a grade-B screenplay to some people (Plot: young girl runs through snow in bare feet to save life!), but it's a true story. And in a lot of ways, it symbolizes how very dangerous and bizarre it's become for homeless kids on America's streets.

I know how tough it is—I've lived there myself. For over 13 years I've lived in the middle of Bedford-Stuyvesant, one of the toughest ghettoes in this country. I've seen a priest shot dead on the sidewalk in front of where we live, by a drug-crazed kid (the kid walked away without a dime).

It's gotten so dangerous I actually carry "mugging money" so I'll have something to give a mugger the next time it happens. We've got three locks on our front door. And a good burglar alarm to boot!

I guess that's interesting in itself—but it's not really the reason I'm telling you this. What's important is if you were to drive through these same streets tonight, you'd see little children like Amy—kids who are 14, 16, 19 years old (and even younger!) who are homeless and alone on the streets.

I get scared for these kids every time I think about that. You really can't believe how awful it is out there for them.

And some of these kids are really just babies. Kids like Gary. . . .

WHAT DO I DO IF A TEEN
I KNOW RUNS AWAY?

Most kids who run away return within 48 hours. Those who stay away can find themselves in many dangerous situations. So do everything you can to bring your child home.

Keep a notebook recording steps you've taken and dates.

Check in with: neighbors, relatives, and your teen's friends, teachers, employer or co-workers.

Contact local hangouts and hospitals.

Call the police. Have an officer come to your house to take a report and pick up recent photos, dental records and fingerprints if available. Get his name, badge number and phone number; the police report number; and the name of the officer who will follow up.

Make sure the police list your teen in the National Crime Information Center (NCIC) computer, and send information to the state clearinghouse on missing children, if there is one in your state.

Contact the National Center for Missing and Exploited Children for help with law enforcement officials— 1-800-843-5678.

Call the Covenant House NINELINE (1-800-999-9999) for support and to check for messages. Leave a message. Also check with any local runaway hotline and the other national runaway hotlines.

Contact runaway shelters locally and in nearby states.

Make posters with photos of your teen listing: age, height, weight, hair and eye color, complexion, physical characteristics (such as scars, birthmarks, braces or pierced ears), circumstances of disappearance, your phone number and police contacts. Distribute these to truck stops, youth-oriented businesses, hospitals, law enforcement agencies.

Be prepared for the first conversation with your teen. Whether in person or by phone, show concern, not anger. Say "I love you."

Prepare to quickly begin resolving the problems which caused your child to leave home. When your child returns home, emotions are likely to run high. Someone outside your family can help deal with these emotions. Planned time for your teen in a temporary residence is sometimes necessary while you are resolving problems. So get outside help from a trained counselor.

Chapter 12
Gary

"Please don't make me leave. I'd rather be tied up and beaten as punishment. Just don't kick me out. I don't want to live out there again. I just can't do it."

Gary hung his head and stared at the old tennis shoes on his feet with mis-matched laces—one lime green and the other fluorescent orange.

He was a kind of funny-looking kid with skinny arms, a long, narrow face, and a barrister's tongue. But there was nothing funny about his life.

He had lived on the streets for years. He'd been hustled and hurt for so long he couldn't bear the thought of going back. Under any circumstances.

There was only one problem. Gary hadn't earned the right to stay at Covenant House. He sat down in the chair, and began pleading his case . . . .

"Hey, I know I'm a problem. I'm sorry . . . I admit it. I guess I fight too much . . . and I know I don't always follow the rules. But wow, I . . . I've had to put up with a lot, too."

"My stepfather used to come in at night after he'd been drinking. He'd just start beating me for no reason at all."

Gary started unbuttoning his dirty blue and white striped shirt. No one asked him to. He just had something he wanted everyone to understand . . . about something he never really understood himself.

"See these?"

Heavy slash marks scarred Gary's upper chest. In case anyone in the room missed the point, he turned sideways in his seat to reveal more scars across his back. "From his belt buckle. From my stepfather's belt buckle."

He paused for a moment, and looked down again at his tennis shoes. It was clear Gary knew he hadn't played by the rules he promised us he'd try to live by. He knew he hadn't fulfilled his part of the covenant—the part that said he would not start fights.

But he wanted—he needed—one more chance.

"Hey, I know I'm a pain sometimes." He leaned forward in his chair. A bony knee poked through a hole in his faded jeans. "But how would you feel? Wouldn't you be a little mad at the world? Wouldn't you feel hurt?"

"And if he wasn't beating me, he told me all the time I was worthless. You know, if someone tells you that often enough, you start to feel it. Guess I didn't let him down, did I?"

For an hour, Gary sat in our office and chronicled—in excruciating detail—the ten solid years of unspeakable physical and emotional abuse heaped on him by his family. Fear danced in his eyes. He spit words out like a machine gun spews out bullets.

Finally, exhausted, he slumped in his seat, his head on his chest, one leg wrapped like a pretzel around the chair leg.

"And do you know what else? My mom just died of AIDS."

He tried to hold back the tears, but he couldn't. "Can you understand why I'm so angry? I'm tryin' my best. But I just don't know how to put it all together. I can't do it. Do you hear me? Nothin's going right. I can't do it."

He's right. Gary can't do it. At least he can't do it alone—which is why we're going to give him another chance. He can stay at Covenant House, as long as he agrees to try to turn his life around—set goals and work at them. And he needs our guidance, love and support to do all that!

That's what it's all about: giving kids a second, third and sometimes fifth chance, if they need it, by understanding the hurt and grief and anger that hang like dark clouds over their lives.

With enough love, Gary, and other kids with similar tragic stories, can put the pieces of their lives back together again.

At least I'm praying he can. You've got to have faith in our kids. You've got to. The moment that dies, their dreams expire, too . . . .

HOW TO MAKE ANGER WORK

Do you ever feel bad about being angry and keep quiet? Though it's easy to say things in anger that you don't mean, anger can also spark talks that will help you and someone you love know each other better. Some guidelines....

When you get mad, **don't blame or accuse**. Say how you feel—annoyed, irritated, upset, etc.—and why. Be specific. Talk facts.

Think solution, not victory. Don't try to "win" arguments.

Stick to the present incident.

Be careful not to attack someone's person or character. Say "I'm furious that you didn't clean up after the mess you made"—not "you're a lazy slob!"

If the situation is touchy, **put your ideas in a letter.** You can say exactly what you mean—and the other person will have time to think it over before answering.

Chapter 13

David

"So what happened to you?" I asked David when I first met him.

"Mumble, mumble, mumble," was all I could make out.

The tall kid's face was bruised and swollen. He tried again but I still couldn't make out what he was saying so he wrote it out for me:

"I got in a fight. My jaw is wired shut."

"Are you feeling all right?" I asked. One nod. "We'll find a place for you to sleep," I told him. "We're really glad you're here. If you need anything you see Estelle, okay?" Another nod.

For three weeks David could only eat liquids through a straw. He ate in Estelle's office because he was ashamed and didn't want the other kids to see him. His conversations with

Estelle consisted of a lot of nods and mumbles.

Estelle found out that David grew up in Mississippi.

His mother told him he had to leave because she had too many other kids to feed and house. At sixteen he was the oldest.

David never knew his father.

For awhile things went well for him at Covenant House. The wires eventually came off, and although he still didn't talk much, we at last got to hear him speak. We even helped him find a job.

One day David got a letter saying his mother had died. He seemed to be okay—too okay. I've learned to worry about kids who seem too okay—usually there's a volcano about to erupt.

The day he was due to get his first paycheck David disappeared.

For two days Estelle asked around, "Have you seen David?" None of the other kids had seen or heard from him. Finally he showed up on the doorstep again. No explanation.

His next paycheck, he disappeared again.

Estelle suspected David was using his paycheck to buy drugs. That's why he stayed away. When he came back again she confronted him, "Are you using drugs, David? Because, you know, if you are, you can't stay at Covenant House."

David denied it and Estelle had to trust him.

The third time it happened we wouldn't let him in. One of our workers called Estelle. Estelle came down and found David sitting on the curb sobbing like a baby. She sat down beside him without saying a word. Minutes passed.

"I was up all night," he finally blurted out. "Doing drugs. Crack. I have a problem. Will you help me?" His confession over, he buried his face in Estelle's lap and wept.

Somehow everything that Covenant House means was wrapped up in that scene. A scared, sad man-child begging for someone, anyone to save him, care about him . . . love him.

Not a perfect kid. Maybe not even a kid you'd be proud to call your own. A kid with problems, big problems.

Let's face it—a kid who can be hard to love. Sort of the way God must feel about all of us sometimes—hard to love.

But God doesn't give up on us. In fact, when we fail the worst He loves the hardest.

He knows we don't have anyone else to turn to.

It's the same with our kids. On the streets David is at the mercy of a very unforgiving city, a city that eats children by the dozen every day.

He doesn't have anyone else to turn to.

"We can help you," Estelle told David. "If you truly want to we can help you get off drugs and stay off."

"Even crack?" he asked. "Even crack," Estelle told him.

Because David admitted he had a problem we let him stay at Covenant House that night and started him in our drug abuse program.

It took some time, but David made real progress.

A few months after he recovered, David enlisted in the Army. He writes Estelle once a week. He's still not very talkative, the letters mostly consist of things like, "I had KP duty this week," and "I made friends with a new guy from Chicago."

Every once in awhile there's a message meant for us. "I'm determined. I really want to show you I can get my life together."

"I know if it weren't for Covenant House, I'd be dead or in jail. Covenant House is all I ever had."

A few weeks ago a tall young man in a crisp Army uniform showed up at Covenant House asking for Estelle. It was David. He was on leave and wanted to come "home." He has changed quite a bit. His hair is shorter and neater. He stands straighter. He says, "Yes, sir," and "No, ma'am." But mostly you see the change in his deep brown eyes. They are clear and purposeful.

Drugs turned David's life upside down, but he had the guts to make it through the program here at Covenant House and put himself right side up again.

David is really proud of himself . . . and so are we.

HOW TO SAY "NO" TO DRINKING AND DRUGS

Let your friends know you're not into drinking and drugs—tell them one at a time so you're not taking on a whole crowd. Your true friends will go along with your decision.

When this won't work, try: "I don't feel like it now," "That junk makes me sick," "That stuff makes me stupid," and "I can't get high—I REALLY want to pass this test so I have to study."

The trick is to state your personal feelings; if your friends feel like you're putting them down, they may think they have to put you down, too, and give YOU a hard time.

Stick to your guns. Some people will give you a hard time about your choices. Let them. The consequences of going along could be harder to deal with than saying no.

Chapter 14
Anthony

"Does your mother work?"

"Yeah, she's a hooker."

"Where does she live?"

"I don't know."

"Does your father work?"

"Not any more. He's dead. He was a pimp."

Denise, our intake counselor, took a deep breath and tried to feel professional. After all, it's her job to interview the kids who come to the Crisis Unit at Covenant House. It's her job to listen to messed-up kids.

But what she heard from Anthony was so bizarre, so sickening, it couldn't be forgotten. This kid's life had been a non-stop, live sex show for 15 years!

But you couldn't tell that from looking at him. He looked a lot like any other 18-year-old with feet that were a little too big, hair that was a little too long, arms that were a little too skinny.

His eyes darted too fast. Every time Denise spoke with him she tried to catch them. After three days his eyes slowed down, locked into hers and the dam burst. You've never seen a kid cry so hard in your life.

His story tumbled out, raging, rushing, swirling.

"They took me and my brother with them. All I remember is dirty hotel rooms and the noises the strange men made when they used my mother. My brother told me not to listen."

Anthony's mother was a prostitute. His father was a pimp. They drifted from town to town, living in cheap motels and rented rooms. They dumped Anthony and his brother on the corner while they "worked."

"What did you have to eat?"

"Not much. Pizza mostly. Soda. We were scared when they didn't come back. We'd get so hungry we'd steal stuff. We'd go into a diner and I'd ask for change and my brother would grab rolls and scraps off the plates."

"Did you go to school?"

"Once in a while, but then we'd move and I wouldn't go."

"Sounds pretty bad. What happened next?"

"They shot my dad. In the face. After that my mother went to pieces. Drugs . . . all kinds of drugs. She'd leave us for three or four days at a time. We stole a lot just to stay alive."

Anthony's brother couldn't take it. He left. A few months later, so did Anthony. He hit the streets . . . a frightened, hungry boy . . . utterly and absolutely alone.

Anthony survived on the street as best he could. Then he met a man who befriended him . . . gave him clothes, good things to eat and a nice room in a big house filled with other boys.

It was great for a few weeks — until one day the man came to Anthony and said, "You have to pay me back."

The house was a prostitution ring. And for the next 2-1/2 years, Anthony "paid the man back" the only way he could — doing tricks two, three, sometimes four times a night.

Why didn't you run away, we wanted to ask Anthony? But we already knew the terrible answer. He was alive, he had food, clothes, his

own room, a little "walking around money."
Why should he leave? Where would he go?
Back to the streets? Back to watching his
mother getting high and entertaining johns?

A 15-year-old prostitute may sound horri-
ble to you, but it was the best life Anthony had
ever experienced!

*(That's the important thing to remember
about these homeless kids. They don't choose
to become homeless — all too often they are
simply abandoned by "parents" who don't
want them, or just don't care. Or they are
abused. Or they are thrown out — literally
thrown out — of their house onto the cold
streets.*

*So, like Anthony, these kids end up alone on
the streets — hungry, tired, cold, desperate,
and scared out of their minds. And they are
sometimes forced to do things — awful, terrible things — just to survive. What else can they
do ... what would you do?)*

There's no telling what might have become
of Anthony if the police had not discovered the
house, raided it and broken up the prostitution
ring. The boys' pimp escaped to another city,
but Anthony found himself homeless again. In
desperation, he came to Covenant House, and

found a place where he was welcomed, loved and wanted — and he didn't have to pay us back.

I think Anthony's going to make it. Today he has a job, and he's working to get his high school General Equivalency Diploma.

I believe he'll stick with it and succeed. It takes a lot of work and patience on the part of our staff and volunteers. It takes a lot of prayers, too.

This poor child's been through enough pain in his life. Every time I think about it, it tears my heart out . . . .

GETTING ALONG WITH YOUR TEEN

Here are some ideas and techniques parents can try to improve their relationship with their teenagers . . . .

Make time for your teen. Find an activity you enjoy doing together and pursue it. If your invitations are declined, keep asking.

Take the long view. Don't treat minor mishaps as major catastrophes. Choose the important issues. Don't make your home a battleground.

Respect your teenager's privacy. If a behavior is worrying you, speak up.

Let your teens sort things out themselves. Never say that you know how your teen feels. They believe their feelings, so new and personal, are unique. They'll learn otherwise — without your help. And never imply that their feelings don't matter or will change. Because teens live in the present, it doesn't matter that they'll soon feel differently.

Don't judge. State facts instead of opinions when you praise or criticize. Stating facts like "Your poem made me smile" or "This report card is all C's and D's!" leaves it up to your teen to draw the appropriate conclusions. Teens are sensitive about being judged positively as well as negatively.

Be generous with praise. Praise your child's efforts, not just accomplishments. And don't comment on the person. "You're a great artist" is hard to live up to. "I loved that drawing" is a fact and comes from your heart.

Set reasonable limits. Teens need them. Your rules should be consistently applied — and rooted in your deepest beliefs and values.

Teach your teen to make sensible decisions and choices by encouraging independence and letting your teenager make mistakes. Don't step in unless you have to.

If you're a parent worried about your kid and need help, call the Covenant House NINELINE, 1-800-999-9999. We'll do our best to help you.

Epilogue
You

I really hope you enjoyed reading this book, and meeting some of our Covenant House kids. I'm grateful you took the time to meet Anthony, and Janice, and Gary, and Michelle and some of the other kids who mean so much to us.

But now, if you don't mind, I'd like to spend just sixty seconds talking about someone else who is also very important to us here — you.

First of all, THANK YOU. Thanks for reading and seeing the life our homeless kids see. For hearing the painful words they too often hear. For experiencing the incredible pain they too often feel.

And I can't possibly end this book without adding one last request — do you think you can become a friend to our kids too? I'm hoping — praying — that when you close the last chapter of this book, you won't be closing the doors on our friendship. Our kids — kids that really and truly are your kids too — need you. They can't live without good people like you.

Last year our Covenant House crisis shelters rescued 28,000 homeless kids from the street ... boys and girls with no family ... kids who are tired, lonely and scared. And we can't continue to reach out and save all these kids, without special help. We need new friends like you.

We simply can't provide the life and death help for these kids without you.

I wish there was an "easy" way to ask a stranger for help. But there isn't. I know you have your own bills to pay, and perhaps you have your own children at home to worry about.

But if there is any way you can reach out now to help a homeless kid, it would be a godsend.

Please ... could you send $15 or $20 or whatever you can afford, so we can save these homeless kids?

We desperately need your help to save these children God has called upon us to save — *truly God's Lost Children.* PLEASE PRAY FOR THESE BOYS AND GIRLS AND HELP US IF YOU CAN. I know if you met them, you'd love them like I do. I just know it. God bless you, and thank you so much for your time, your prayers, and your support.

In God's love,
Sister Mary Rose McGeady
President, Covenant House

HOW YOU CAN HELP

Become politically streetwise. Contact your elected officials. They respond to appropriate, positive pressure. Impress upon them the importance of passing laws which will help preserve the family unit and safeguard youngsters from being victimized by substance abuse, pornography, and other forms of exploitation.

Urge churches, synagogues, and service clubs to address the plight of homeless and exploited kids. Make sure your pastors, rabbis, and community leaders confront the elements which cause homelessness. See that they involve their congregations and clubs in these issues. Their support is crucial in helping families stay together. They can help provide the guidance which will dissuade youngsters from turning to alcohol and drugs.

You can be a crucial force in your own family, your neighborhood, your community in combatting those forces that seek to exploit homeless youngsters.

Counter these forces by helping to strengthen the family and your neighborhood community. Do it early and often. Ask your churches and schools to help if you aren't able.

If you're a parent worried about your kid and need help, call the Covenant House NINELINE, 1-800-999-9999. We'll do our best to assist you.

A Gift To Be Embraced

Reflections on the
Covenant House Faith Community

*The following was written by Alec As-
pinwall, a former member of the Covenant
House Faith Community in New York City.*

Even after making the decision to visit the
Covenant House Faith Community in New
York City, I have to admit I was still somewhat
suspicious. The closer I got to the address on
Eighth Avenue in the heart of Times Square, in
fact, the more my questions grew. What would
draw normal people away from their comfortable lifestyles to pray for three hours a day and
work with street kids while making $12 a
week? What was drawing me?

For some time I had been searching for a
way to deepen my relationship with God, and

there was certainly something pushing me to take a closer look. Now, that courage seemed foolish and even a little frightening as I stood on the doorstep waiting for someone to answer the bell. I tried to look nonchalant, but as I glanced across the street, my eyes read the invitation posted on the door of the porno theater and I turned away in disgust — but without success. All around me, as I looked to the left and then to the right, the sorry sights and sounds of a string of "adult entertainment centers" made my stomach turn. I felt stunned. Is this where I had to live if I wanted to feel closer to God? Was I crazy? The eyes of the street people told me what I already knew. "You don't belong here," they said. They were right. I didn't belong here.

Then the door opened, and I was met with a warm smile. I tried to contain my gratitude for the timely rescue.

Once inside I was surprised by the size of the dwelling. It consisted of two six-story buildings joined by a large chapel. The dormitory-style living was neither elegant nor impoverished, but quite plain. The people I was soon to meet, however, were anything but plain.

I found myself in the midst of a Christian "melting pot." There were nurses, teachers, nuns, businesspeople, laborers, retired mothers, and recent college graduates. They had come from all over the country and even from abroad. Although Catholic in prayer and worship, the Community also had members from various Christian denominations. There were conservatives and liberals, rich and not so rich, young and the young at heart. Each had a different story to tell as to why they had come to Covenant House, but their differences were united by the call to strengthen their relationship with one God. To do so, they were willing to accept the challenge of intense prayer (three hours a day), communal living, and working with the kids of Covenant House, whose lifestyle on the street can make them pretty tough to deal with at times. They hurt so much that sometimes the only way they can feel better about themselves is to hurt you instead.

I had also expected Community members to be a solemn bunch, bearing the weight of the pervasive tragedy that surrounded them — but I found just the opposite to be true. The Community had a vibrant spirit that was full of life and laughter. Somehow the pain they were

daily exposed to had actually made room for
joy. I'm not saying that I didn't perceive their
own suffering, for many of them shared with
me the struggles they were experiencing with
the kids of Covenant House and with themselves.   But they were beginning to see their
struggle no longer as a punishment to be en-
dured, but as a gift to be embraced. I began to
think that there might be something to that line
from the Gospel about how "dying to yourself
will bring new life."

By the end of the week, I had a lot to think
and pray about. Was I ready to commit to a
minimum of 13 months of three hours a day of
prayer? Could I dedicate myself to a simple
lifestyle in a chaste community? Was I able to
let go of the stability offered by my loved ones
and my career? Was I willing to be sent to any
one of the Covenant House sites assigned to me
and work at any job, whether it was working
directly with the kids or not? Most of all, could
I really love those hardened street kids and let
myself be touched by their pain?

I went home to California and asked God to
give me a sign. Something simple. An eclipse
maybe! No sign came. What did come, finally,
was a sense of peace that told me it was alright

to go against all the norms and ambitions ingrained in me and take a step forward in faith. After receiving a letter from the Orientation Director, I gave notice at my job and began to make plans to come back to New York.

It's hard to believe I've been here a year now. I've learned so much about myself, the kids, and God. I've learned, for instance, that drawing closer to God is a constant challenge and process. Street kids, I've come to learn, really have soft centers underneath those hard exteriors, and they often have more to teach me than I them. And God is always there, even though sometimes I don't recognize Him.

I still don't like the neighborhood, and I still get the same stares on the street that I did a year ago. Only now, sometimes I see Christ behind the cold eyes, and He reassures me, "You do belong here."

If you would like more information about joining the Faith Community, please write to Orientation Director of Faith Community, 346 West 17th Street, New York, NY 10011-5002, or call (212) 727-4000.

Need expert support or referral?

*Call our NINELINE counselors
at 1-800-999-9999.*

*We'll put you in touch with
people who can help you right
in your hometown.*

1-800-999-9999

This call is free.

NOTES

NOTES

> *"I bound myself by oath, I made a covenant with you . . . and you became mine."*   **Ezekiel 16:8**

The only way to stop the pain and degradation of street children is to get more people involved in solutions to the devastating problems they face every night of their lives.

After you read this book, please pass it along to a friend. If you would like more copies, just fill out this coupon and return it to us in the envelope provided. And know that because you took the time to care, a kid won't have to sell himself to survive tonight.

Please send me _____ copies of *God's Lost Children*. To help defray the cost of sending you these books, we request a minimum donation of $5 per book.

Name _____

Address _____

City _____ State _____ Zip _____

Please make your check payable to Covenant House.
Your gift is tax deductible.

Many people like to charge their gift. If you would like to, please fill out the information below:

I prefer to charge my: _____ MasterCard _____ Visa

Account # _____

Amount _____ Exp. Date _____

Signature _____

Mail to: **Covenant House**
JAF Box 2973
New York, NY 10116-2973   FBKONZ

Or, call 1-800-388-3888 to charge your gift on your MasterCard or Visa or to get more information.

"I bound myself by oath, I made a covenant with you . . . and you became mine."   **Ezekiel 16:8**

Covenant House depends almost entirely on gifts from friends like you to help 28,000 homeless and runaway children every year. We provide food, clothing, shelter, medical attention, educational and vocational training, and counseling to kids with no place to go for help. Please help if you can.

YES! I want to help the kids at Covenant House.
Here is my gift of: ☐ $10 ~ ☐ $20   ☐ $25   ☐ **Other**

Name _____

Address _____

City _____ **State** _____ **Zip** _____

Please make your check payable to Covenant House.
Your gift is tax deductible.

Many people like to charge their gift. If you would like to, please fill out the information below:

I prefer to charge my: ____**MasterCard** ____**Visa**

Account # _____

Amount _____ **Exp. Date** _____

Signature _____

Mail to: Covenant House
                JAF Box 2973
                New York, NY 10116-2973   FBCPNZ

Or, call 1-800-388-3888 to charge your gift.

Copies of our financial and operating reports have been filed with the state and are available on request. To obtain one, simply write: NY Department of State, Charities Registration Section, 162 Washington Ave., Albany, NY 12231 or Covenant House, JAF Box 2973, New York, NY 10116-2973.

WV RESIDENTS: A copy of the official registration and supporting documents may be obtained from West Virginia Secretary of State, State Capitol, Charleston, WV 25305.